The Mississippi

KENTUCKY

TENNESSEE

ILLINOIS

Cairo

New Madrid

Memphis

MISSOURI

MISSISSIPPI

YAZOO

Vicksburg

Delta

Arkansas City

Natchez

Little Rock

ARKANSAS

LOUISIANA

NESHIO

OKLAHOMA

RED

TEXAS

FLORIDA

Nashville

CUMBERLAND

OHIO

TENNESSEE

ALABAMA

ALABAMA

Montgomery

Birmingham

TOMBIGBEE

GULF OF MEXICO

New Orleans

DELTA

Baton Rouge

MISSISSIPPI

Atchafalaya

MISSISSIPPI

WHITE

OUACHITA

ARKANSAS

SABINE

Km 0   100   200
M 0   50   100   150

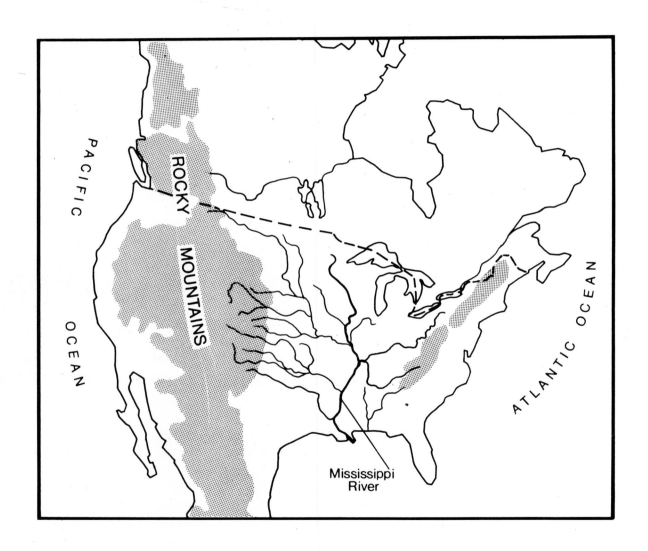

PACIFIC

OCEAN

ROCKY

MOUNTAINS

ATLANTIC OCEAN

Mississippi
River

The Mississippi

The Indians of North America were the first to call this river the Mississippi, meaning great river. Today it is great not only in size but also in importance as a transport system for the heavy industries of the United States.

In this book we follow the Mississippi from its source as a small stream near the Canadian border to its great muddy delta in the Gulf of Mexico. We look at its towns and people, its place in the history of exploration and slavery, its wildlife, and the work of engineers who have struggled to overcome this vast, restless giant of a river.

Frontispiece   *A Mississippi paddleboat, the* Delta Queen

Rivers of the World

The Mississippi

Susan Darell-Brown

Wayland/Silver Burdett

Rivers of the World

Amazon
Colorado
Congo
Danube
Ganges
Mississippi
Nile
Rhine
St Lawrence
Thames
Volga
Yellow River

Copyright © 1979 Wayland (Publishers) Limited.
First published in 1979 by
Wayland Publishers Limited
61 Western Road, Hove,
Sussex BN3 1JD, England
ISBN 0 85340 454 2
Second impression 1985

Published in the United States by
Silver Burdett Company, Morristown,
New Jersey.
1985 printing.
ISBN 0 382 06204 3
Library of Congress Catalog Card Number 78-62982

Phototypeset by Trident Graphics Ltd., Reigate, Surrey
Printed in Italy by G. Canale & C.S.p.A., Turin

Contents

The mighty Mississippi 9
At the source 15
Minneapolis and St. Paul 21
Sailing to St. Louis 25
Mississippi past and present 33
Into the South 39
Memphis to Baton Rouge 47
New Orleans and the Delta 55
Glossary 62
Further Reading 63
Facts and figures 64
Index 65

The great river channel of the upper Mississippi

The mighty Mississippi

Red Indians lived in North America for thousands of years before the first Europeans arrived there. It was a Red Indian tribe – the Chippewa – who called this great wide river the Misi Sipi, meaning "Big Water". It is a good name, for the Mississippi is long as well as wide. It winds for 3,800 km (2,375 miles) through the United States of America, cutting the land in two from a point near the Canadian border all the way south to the Gulf of Mexico.

The first European to see the Mississippi called it the Rio Grande, which also means "Big River". Later, Negro slaves in the South called it Old Man River, Old Devil River and Old Al (short for alligator).

The Mississippi, with its hundreds of tributaries, gathers water from a huge area. Although it starts as a small stream, by the time it reaches half-way along its journey to the sea it is a great waterway nearly 1½ km (1 mile) wide. For most of the year it is quite tame, but when the early spring rains start to fall and the snows melt in the high mountains, the water rises.

Above *View from space of the junction of the Mississippi (top) with the Missouri (below) at St. Louis*

Then it shows its great power. People watch closely to see if it is going to get too high and flood the land.

But the Mississippi has not always been such a long river. Millions of years ago the whole

9

Mississippi basin was part of the Gulf of Mexico. Slowly the area filled up with a mixture of clays, sands and rocks left behind by Ice Age glaciers. When the ice melted at the end of the last Ice Age, huge lakes were formed, including the Great Lakes of North America. The lakes in Northern Minnesota are the remains of other lakes formed at this time. One of these is Lake Itasca, from which the Mississippi is thought to rise.

The Mississippi itself created the land in between the Appalachian Mountains to the east and the Rocky Mountains to the west. For thousands of years the river left rich silt behind, so slowly the land was built up. Because of this the countryside is fairly flat. These vast fertile plains are very good for growing crops.

The main tributary of the Mississippi system is the Missouri, which rises high in the Rocky Mountains. The Missouri travels nearly 4,000 km (2,500 miles) before it joins the Mississippi. The two rivers together – the Mississippi and the Missouri – make up what is claimed to be the longest waterway in the world: approximately 6,400 km (4,000 miles).

The first European to see the Mississippi was a Spaniard, Hernando de Soto. He landed in Florida and made his way west with an army of

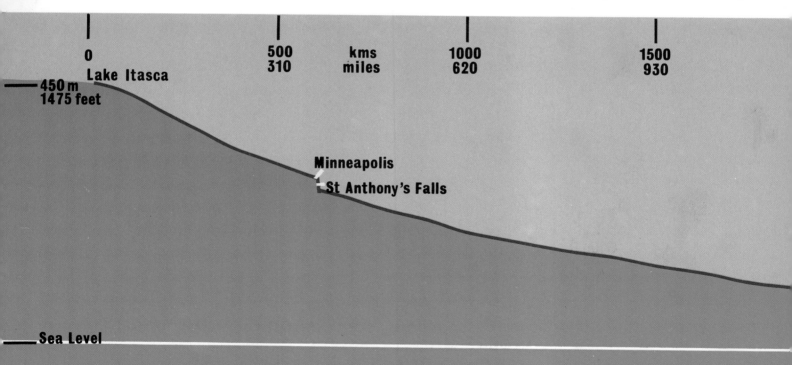

A cross-section diagram of the Mississippi from its source to the Gulf of Mexico

730 men, in search of gold and precious stones. In 1541 he came to a very large muddy river, so broad that he could hardly see across; he called it Rio Grande. De Soto never found gold, only mosquitoes which gave him malaria. In 1542 he died. On hearing of his fate, others were not encouraged to follow him.

So it was not until 1673 that other "white men" saw the Mississippi. Two Frenchmen, Louis Jolliet and Jacques Marquette, were sent from Quebec in Canada to explore the area near the source of the river. It was thought the river might run from east to west. If so, it would make a good trade route. They journeyed down the

| 2500 | | 3000 | | 3500 | kms | 4000 |
| 1550 | | 1860 | | 2170 | miles | 2480 |

St Louis

Cairo

New Orleans

Above *Thomas Jefferson, third president of the United States, who bought Louisiana from the French*

Wisconsin River by canoe, joined the Mississippi and went on down to where the city of Arkansas lies today. Having found that the river ran north to south, not east to west, they returned to Quebec.

In 1681 another Frenchman, Robert Cavalier, went all the way down to the river mouth, setting up forts on the way. In 1718 Jean Baptiste Le Moyne founded New Orleans. Four years later it was the largest town on the Mississippi.

New Orleans belonged to the French until 1764 when it was given to the Spanish by the French king, Louis XV. It remained Spanish for thirty-six years before returning to the French. Finally, in 1803, Napoleon Bonaparte sold it, along with the territory then called Louisiana, to the American president, Thomas Jefferson. The price was fifteen million dollars. This, the largest sale of land in history, became known as the Louisiana Purchase. So the whole river became part of the United States.

Up to the end of the nineteenth century, nothing much had been done to control the river. Every spring, floods ruined crops and farms — sometimes covering whole towns. The people who lived there became disheartened and moved away. Not only did the river flood; it also changed its course. What one year was a field, farm or town, the next was the bed of the river. It was too expensive to do anything to stop this. However, the United States government finally set aside money for the taming of the river. Dams, dykes, locks and canals have been built in their hundreds to control the waters. Now every section of the river is checked to ensure no damage is done to the valuable crops or the towns within range of the river in flood.

Today the Mississippi is a vital transport system for American industry. Tugs push great barges carrying oil, petrol, coal, iron, sand, limestone, sulphur, chemicals, ores, grain and building materials. It is slow but cheap to take them this way. One tug can push up to forty barges carrying cargo which otherwise would fill a thousand freight train wagons.

Above *Louis Jolliet and Jacques Marquette being helped by Indians on their hazardous journey along the unknown waters of the Mississippi in 1673* 13

Above *Lake Itasca, the peaceful source of the mighty Mississippi*

At the source

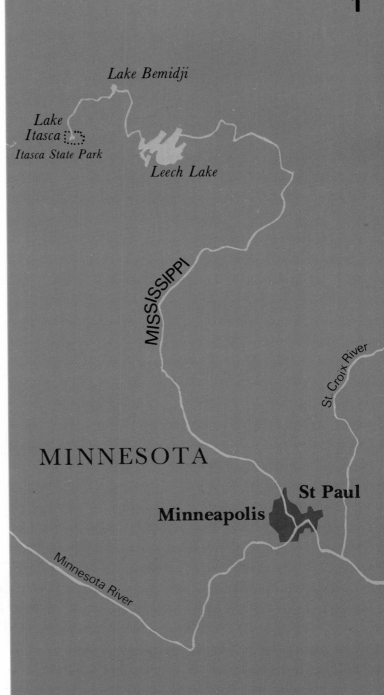

1

The Mississippi is thought to rise from Lake Itasca, a small lake surrounded by pine trees in a remote part of Minnesota. Minnesota is known as the state of 10,000 lakes, although this is an understatement. There are in fact over 15,000.

The land around Lake Itasca has been made into a State Park, so we have to get permission from the authorities to go there. This is a perfect place for camping and all the things that go with it: boating, fishing, water-skiing, walking and skating in winter.

In the days when Red Indians were the only people living in the area it was even more of a wilderness, dangerous and difficult for explorers. It was not until about 1832 that Henry Rowe Schoolcraft found a small lake, called it Lake Itasca and announced that it was the true source of the Mississippi. This was accepted as true for a long time, but there are so many lakes nearby that it is difficult to be absolutely sure.

This part of the country is where the fur trappers used to make their living. They would spend the winters catching animals and then take the skins, by river, to trading posts. One of their main catches was the beaver. These busy little animals can still be seen today, gnawing through trees, building dams and underwater houses. Deer, moose and black bear still live here too. Sadly, the buffalo have been killed off by the Indians and early settlers who hunted buffalo for meat and skins. The loon is the Minnesota state bird and its eerie, wolf-like cry can be heard as we travel.

16 **Above left** *Jim Baker, a famous trapper, wearing an Indian pouch and knife*

Above right *A young fawn hides in the grass*

paddle downstream but we are not going south. For the first 100 km (63 miles) or so the river takes us north-east, through swamp, forest and green pasture. After passing through Lake Bemidji it begins to look more like the large river we expected. It is now 70 m (230 ft) wide and flowing south.

This whole area of the northern US through which we are passing has many dairy farms, so it is called the Dairy Belt. Corn, maize and soybeans are grown as well, but this type of country – rolling hills and rich grassland – is perfect for cows.

As you would expect, with so many pine trees around, this is also logging country, where trees are cut down for timber. We shall see logs being floated downstream like huge rafts to sawmills near Minneapolis. Fisheries have also been set up in this early stretch of the river. The water is clean and the authorities are intent on keeping it so. The fish are mainly bass, carp, walleye, suckers and catfish which are caught for sport and food.

Just before reaching Minneapolis, the first large city on our journey, we leave the river to join one of two canals which have been built to avoid St. Anthony's Falls. These falls are 22 m (70 ft) high. The rock they tumble over is made of limestone which is soft and easily worn away by fast-flowing water. At the beginning of this century it was wearing away so fast that the lip of the falls had to be artificially strengthened with concrete.

When the river leaves Lake Itasca it is only about 3 m (10 ft) wide and 10 cm (4 in) deep, so we shall start our journey in canoes. The Indians made canoes from tree bark, but modern ones are made of aluminium. The water is clear and bright; slowly the river begins to widen. We

The Mississippi flowing through St. Paul

Minneapolis and St. Paul

Minneapolis and St. Paul are known as the Twin Cities, but they are not identical twins. Minneapolis, a very modern city, is on the west bank; St. Paul, a more old-fashioned city, is on the east. Half the population of the state of Minnesota live in these two cities, so the houses spread out over a large area.

The first European settlers in this part of America came mainly from Germany, Norway, Sweden, Finland, Denmark and Ireland. They logged the white-pine forests, mined the iron ore, and started farming its prairies. To do all this they had to help one another. Their descendants have much the same helpful attitude to life to this day.

They have built their cities with beautiful parks. These cities are pleasant places to live, with fewer traffic jams, less poverty and violent crime than most other American cities. The people have given many millions of dollars to cultural and other development in the cities as well as throughout the state. People from all over Minnesota come here for the theatre, music, dance, art and education. Minneapolis may be the more modern city, but it is St. Paul that is the seat of the state's government. St. Paul has many museums full of treasures and is extremely proud of its heritage. The weather in Minnesota is very cold in winter, with lots of snow. But it is easy to go shopping in Minneapolis without being out of doors very often. In the town centre the buildings are linked together by covered walkways, all heated, so it is possible to be in your shirt-sleeves in the middle of winter.

When the lakes are frozen, the people go skating, iceboating, snowmobiling, skiing, and fishing through the ice. In the old days they had teams of dogs pulling sledges; now they have the snowmobile, a machine rather like a bumper-car on skis, which was invented by a Minnesotan. Another invention by a Minnesotan is the water-ski.

These two cities became one of the gateways to the West in the days of the early settlers. First the river was crossed by boats; then came the railway with its bridges. There are seventeen bridges now, both rail and road. Minneapolis is the chief railway centre of the north-west. Here we will also find the Grain Exchange. The price for grain is decided in this central exchange. The farmers from all around listen to the radio to see whether it is worth taking their grain to market, or whether they should wait for prices to rise.

The Mississippi becomes navigable by larger

boats here and we will find the first dam in a
series of twenty-seven between Minneapolis and
St. Louis. These have all been built to keep the
river open to shipping.

We continue our journey by barge, by special
invitation from the captain. His tugboat will
push, not pull, a long chain of barges all linked
together, sometimes three abreast. These tug-
boats are fitted with all the most modern aids.

The captain does not have to guess whether
there is a new sandbank or blockage in the river,
for his instruments tell him. All the same, it is
still a very skilled job to take a cargo of this size
on the Mississippi. At certain points it is too narrow for a wide load, so he has to untie the
barges, leave half of them anchored, take half
ahead, go back for the others and then link them
all up again.

Above *Logs are floated down to Minneapolis from the* 23
north

Above *The junction of the St. Croix river and the Mississippi*

Sailing to St. Louis

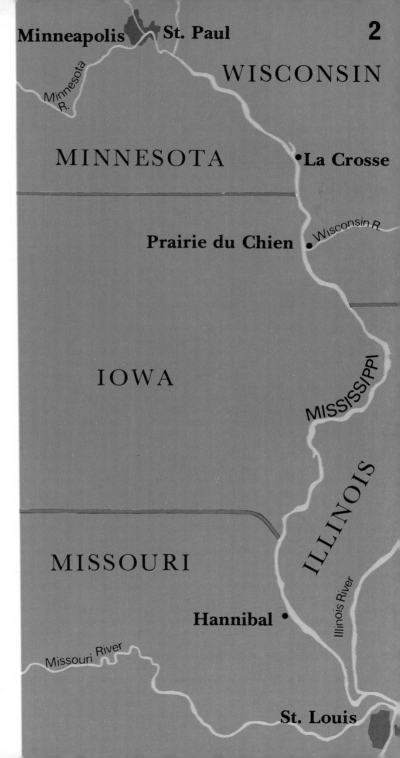

2

Up to now the Mississippi has been much like other rivers. Now we begin to see why it is so important. The force of the water has, over the years, cut a wide route between rocky cliffs. It is as if nature had built its own walls to keep the water in. As our barges make their way slowly downriver we can sit back and wonder at the beauty of the countryside passing by.

This stretch of the river is very attractive. The Minnesota River joins us from the right; the St. Croix River from the left. There are islands and sandbanks. Here we shall be able to see herons, cranes and eagles, but the water is no longer as clean as it was before Minneapolis. The tributaries joining it bring silt and mud and the boats and towns along its course pollute it, but it still has charm.

Since shortly after Minneapolis the river has been the boundary between the states of Minnesota and Wisconsin. South of La Crosse we leave Minnesota on the right bank and enter Iowa, "The Beautiful Land" as it was called by

the Indians. For most of its course the Mississippi provides a convenient boundary between the states, but this raises difficulties further downstream, as we shall see.

Prairie du Chien, Wisconsin, was a fur trappers' station in the early days. The house of one of the fur-buying agents, John Jacob Astor, is open to the public and is well worth a visit. It is a grand house called Villa Louis and will give us some idea of how luxurious life was for those who made themselves rich from the fur trade.

Across the river at McGregor we can visit the Effigy Mounds National Monument. These are the ritual burial barrows of the Moundbuilders, the chief Indian tribe of the Mid-west before Columbus discovered America. The mounds are shaped like animals, the largest being like a bear.

About 240 km (150 miles) before St. Louis, round one of the many bends, we reach a town called Hannibal. It was here that Mark Twain, the American writer, was born in 1835 and here he spent his childhood. Of course the town has grown about six times larger now but the memory of this great American writer is still preserved. We can visit his house at 206 Hill Street. Part of the town has been restored to look as it did some 125 years ago.

Mark Twain loved the Mississippi. When he was a child he spent as much time as he could playing by it, in it and on it. He listened to the stories of the river pilots and and was hypnotized by the mystery of the river. Mark Twain was not the name he was born with; his real name was Samuel Langhorne Clemens. His pen name was taken from the cry "mark twain" heard in his steamboat days, meaning two fathoms of water beneath the boat, a navigable depth. The word "mark" means the mark on the rope used for taking the depth. "Twain" means two.

He wrote many books; the ones which were inspired by his life on the Mississippi are *The Adventures of Tom Sawyer, Life on the Mississippi* and *The Adventures of Huckleberry Finn.* Huckleberry Finn went down the river on a raft, and a dangerous voyage it was.

We rejoin our barge and continue in the relative safety of modern technology. The river is now full of barges making their way to and fro with their various cargoes. We have reached the corn-growing area. The fields stretch as far as the eye can see. A huge amount of maize is grown here, particularly in Illinois, for the heavy rainfall and dark-grey soil suit it. It is grown not as food for people but for pigs and other livestock. To the west are some of the finest wheat-growing lands in the world. The number and variety of machines involved in farming these

Below *Like a modern Tom Sawyer or Huck Finn, this boy fishes in the Mississippi*

lands is something to behold. During the harvest it is not unusual to see six to a dozen combine harvesters spread out across the landscape devouring the crops like giant locusts.

Just before we get to Grafton, the Illinois River joins us from the east. This flows from Lake Michigan and is the Mississippi's link with the Great Lakes. A few miles further on, the mighty Missouri joins us from the west, a little way north of St. Louis. The Missouri is nick-

named "The Big Muddy" and is true to its name. It rises high in the Rocky Mountains to the west and has covered a much greater distance than the Mississippi by the time they meet. It is so muddy because it flows very fast. On its way it tears into the earth carrying the soil downstream. In one year it washes 100 million tonnes of rich earth into the Mississippi. A tremendous amount of work has been done by the Missouri River Authority to control these waters

Below   *A maize sheller in Iowa, eating its way through the fields*

Above *Lewis and Clark, in canoes, are spotted by Indians*

but a good deal more has still to be completed. At present you can sail up the Missouri only as far as Kansas City.

Now we arrive at St. Louis which today is an important industrial city. It was once the gateway to the West for settlers. Until the Louisiana Purchase, in 1803, St. Louis was a small French outpost, used only by trappers and river boatmen. In 1804, President Jefferson sent two men, Merriweather Lewis and William Clark, to explore westward and find a route to the Pacific. When they returned with maps and stories of the exciting country they had found, people started to flock to St. Louis.

Above *A wagon train preparing to leave St. Louis for the west*

From here hundreds of hopeful settlers set out in search of new and better lives. The land to the west was what they called "free land", because it did not belong to anyone, except the Indians. If the settlers could reach it, then it was theirs. In St. Louis they bought wagons, supplies and horses, joined a wagon train and set off on their adventurous and often very dangerous journey across the western plains. There were many dangers. Large numbers of people died on the journey, some of cholera, some of exhaustion; some were killed by Indians and some found it impossible to cross the great mountains of the Rockies and Sierra Nevada. But many achieved their goal and settled in California and Oregon.

As we enter St. Louis we see an enormous steel arch 192 m (630 ft) high, which has been built to symbolize this gateway to the West. It stands close to the river and is so large that there are capsule-like trains inside which take visitors to an observation tower. From here you can see across the city to the plains beyond.

Above *The vast Gateway Arch at St. Louis. Visitors can travel to the top to look out at the surrounding* countryside

31

A flat-boat on the Mississippi in the early nineteenth century

Mississippi past and present

Although the Missouri, the "Big Muddy", has now joined the Mississippi, and the river is wider still, there is no real change in the landscape until we get to Cairo.

For a while we can sit and dream of days gone by and imagine the river full of steamboats and the craft used to move goods. There were many attempts at making boats suitable for use on the Mississippi. In 1796 some Dutch settlers built a strange craft with oars worked by eight horses treading in a circle, but this was wrecked by a strong current. Large canoes with masts and other boats with oars and sails were tried.

The most usual form of transport, however, was the barge. Of course, these had no engines. They floated downstream to New Orleans, using sails for the return journey. With the coming of the steam era these barges could not compete with the steamboat. By 1830 there were 1,200 steamboats arriving at New Orleans. The new ships went at a speed of 12 knots downstream and 5 knots upstream. This was faster than any other craft.

Journeys on the river were full of excitement and adventure. Races often took place between steamers. These races were a great attraction. The captains were proud men and each was convinced that his skill was greater than any other man's on the river. The passengers urged the captains on, not caring about the danger. Sometimes the ships' boilers exploded through overheating and the boats sank. Hundreds of people were killed each year but the races still went on. It was not always through racing that boats were lost. The boats were made of wood, so fires were common; sometimes they would hit a reef and sink. The average life of a steamboat was five years. Most of them met a violent end.

A midnight race between steamboats

It was in these early days that the Mississippi was used as a border between states, and it was on the stretch between Illinois and Missouri, where we are now, that this proved to be most difficult. Before the American Civil War, when slavery was allowed in Missouri but not in Illinois, problems arose whenever the river changed its course. One day Negroes in Missouri would be slaves; the next day they might, in theory, be in Illinois and therefore free men. So it was decided that the river changed its course too often and could no longer be used as a boundary.

At Cairo the Ohio River meets the Mississippi. Now the river changes its character. An enormous quantity of water is brought to it by

The Delta Queen, *clearly showing the paddle wheel at the stern and the gang plank in front*

the Ohio. The Mississippi becomes rougher and more cruel. The Ohio rises in the mountains of Pennsylvania and gathers water all along its course from the Appalachian Mountains. These mountains cause heavy rainfall regularly all year so it is easy to see why the quantity of water in the Ohio River is so great. It became clear that control of these rivers and their tributaries was essential, so authorities were set up to deal with the problem. The Tennessee Valley River Authority (TVA) is one of these and is an example which many other river authorities all over the world have followed.

The Tennessee River is the last and the largest tributary to join the Ohio before it reaches the Mississippi. The TVA, set up in 1933, was put in charge of developing and conserving the river and the whole area of land drained by it. It is an area about the size of England and Scotland together. The river had to be kept open for shipping for 1,050 km (650 miles) from the Tennessee's junction with the Ohio River as far upstream as Knoxville. Also, the flood waters had to be controlled, so a vast stairway of nine dams was built, each with locks for shipping. Further upstream other dams were made, mainly to produce hydro-electric power. These included the highest dam in the eastern United States – the 150 m (500 ft) high Fontana Dam on the Little Tennessee River.

Before the TVA was set up, the land was hardly used; farming was almost unknown and forests were cut down and burned. The people were very poor and suffered greatly from malaria. This disease is passed into human bodies by mosquitoes whose larvae live in shallow water. It has now been wiped out from the area by regularly raising and lowering the water level about 30 cm (1 ft) at the many dams. This process dries out the shallows, killing the mosquito larvae. With healthy people the farming has prospered, woodlands have been planted, nature reserves have been made and industries set up. People can also go fishing, boating, camping, water-skiing and so on. The story of the TVA is a remarkable success story.

Above *A canal and lock in the Tennessee Valley River Authority area*

Rescue operations in flooded Louisiana, after a hurricane

Into the South

Below the Corn Belt we come to an area of warm climate where various crops are grown. Here large quantities of tobacco are produced. Tobacco, together with the cotton, rice and sugar cane of the Deep South, used to be looked after by the Negro slaves. It was the slaves who improved these lands and made them fit for crops. They drained marshes, cut down cypress trees to build houses on the plantations and dug the first ditches. Their hard work, forced on them by their masters, created the rich, white "cotton barons" of the 1830–60 period.

The other crop we see growing is the groundnut, more commonly known as the peanut. The peanut is an example of how we can take things for granted. When you buy a packet of nuts, do you ever stop to think how they grow? As you might guess from its name, the groundnut is actually formed under the soil. The flower of the plant puts its head down to the ground, where it forms the pod with the nut-like seeds inside.

South of Cairo, the river banks have been built up, sometimes to a height of over 20 m (60 ft) to

Cotton being loaded onto a steamboat through a chute

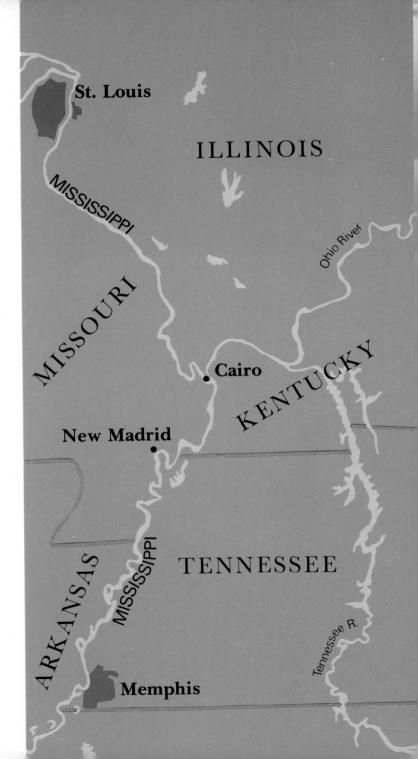

hold back the flood waters. Towns are less frequent and the landscape less interesting. The people got tired of building towns only to have them swept away or ruined by the flooding river. So they moved away, further inland.

Not far south of Cairo is New Madrid. This is really "New New Madrid" for the original town now lies under the river-bed, with boats and barges passing over it. This town was destroyed after a large earthquake in 1811. The Mississippi changed course and swallowed up the city and a huge area round it.

Many other early towns have been destroyed. Kaskasia (the original capital of Illinois) and a town called Napoleon, are now buried deep in mud. The Mississippi's changes of direction produce some strange results. Towns and houses built on the river's edge may find themselves far inland. Those built inland sometimes end up on the river's edge!

At Memphis we are in the Cotton Belt. The growth of cotton was started because of the American War of Independence in the 1770s. Because of the war, materials could no longer be imported from England, so the American people started growing their own cotton. Hundreds more slaves were imported and enormous areas planted. Men became rich from this and built beautiful plantation houses. Some of these can be seen from the river as we travel downstream.

In Memphis we begin to hear the old songs of the South and become aware of the slower pace of life. In the southern states, as in all warm

Evening at the riverside, Memphis

42   *Cotton picking as it used to be. This old picture shows slaves on a plantation by the river, with a steamboat in the distance*

Cotton picking as it is done today

climates, the people take life more easily. They work hard, but there does not seem to be the same urgency as in the colder northern climate. Even the way of speaking is slower – what is known as the "southern drawl".

Memphis is the centre of the cotton trade. Our barge will probably exchange some of its grain cargo for cotton or tobacco to be taken down to New Orleans.

It is sometimes thought that a wide river must

also be a deep river. This is not always true; it is certainly not so in the case of the Mississippi. Remember, the river runs down a wide flat valley, sloping very gently. When flowing slowly it gradually drops the silt which has been brought down from the hills. So the silt fills up the river bottom and builds itself up into raised banks (levees) along the river side.

To keep shipping moving at all times, a channel 3 m (10 ft) deep and 100 m (110 yds) wide has to be kept clear. This is done by dredging.

We shall see quite a few of these strange-looking dredgers at work clearing a pathway through the silt. These boats look like huge vacuum cleaners. They have a long pipe which is floated on wooden supports and goes from the boat to the bank of the river. The boat sucks up the silt and mud from the river-bed and pumps it through the pipe.

We shall also see snag boats. These are used to remove floating trees and any other obstructions which could be a danger to river traffic.

Below *A baby alligator riding on its mother's back*

45

46   *The* Sultana *steamboat disaster. When the boilers exploded the ship caught fire and more than 1,500 people lost their lives*

Memphis to Baton Rouge

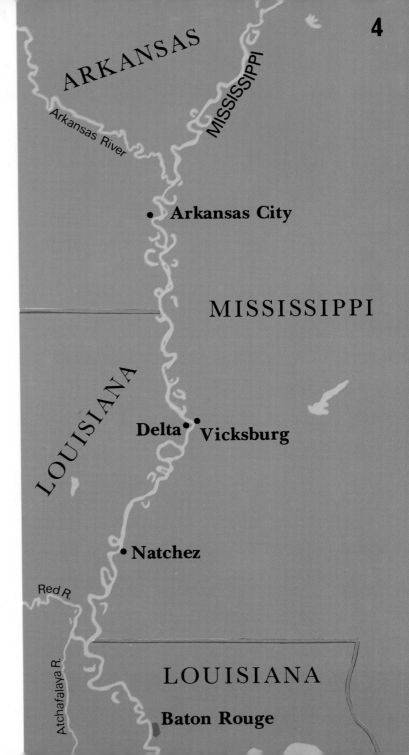

On and on the river winds along its seemingly endless journey. It is easy to see why it has been nicknamed "the crookedest river in the world". The engineers have straightened it out quite a bit – in fact by some 245 km (152 miles) – in their attempt to get the water to the sea as quickly as possible. But it still twists and turns.

Just south of Memphis we come to the border between Tennessee and Mississippi on the left bank. Arkansas (pronounced Ark-an-saw) is to the right. Beneath a farm in Arkansas lies the wreck of the *Sultana*. The destruction of this ship was the worst navigational disaster of all time. It was at the end of the American Civil War in the 1860s when hundreds of Northern troops were returning home. The ship was built to hold a thousand people but over two thousand crowded aboard. Shortly after leaving Memphis, the *Sultana* exploded and 1,550 soldiers were drowned. This is more than the number of people lost when the great *Titanic* sank in 1912.

Above Arkansas city, the Arkansas River joins

the Mississippi, making it even wider. The town of Delta, which was once almost 5 km (3 miles) downstream from Vicksburg, we now find about 3 km (2 miles) *before* Vicksburg. The town has not moved – the river has changed its course.

It is at Vicksburg that we see the full extent of the work which has been done on the Mississippi in an attempt to tame the giant river. Here there is a scale model of the whole of the Mississippi basin. Every dam, dyke and levee is represented: the mountains, streams, basin contours, every aspect is there. The model, which covers a very large area, is used to help engineers in their fight to control the river. They can flood parts of the model to see what would happen to the real river at any point if the waters rose too high. There are laboratories where engineers can study photograph taken from aeroplanes and satellites as well as information on geology (rock structure) taken from drillings and soundings.

The engineers have thought up the worst possible weather they can imagine, with all elements at their most dangerous at the same time. So long as nothing totally unexpected happens, the Mississippi should remain harmless to the people living by it. It seems that the battle against the river has finally been won, but only time will tell if this is really true.

Further downstream is the city of Natchez. Here we are reminded of the days when the wealthy plantation owners moved into town every year for the "season": the time of parties and merry-making. We can still see the large,

48   **Above**   *A Little Egret wading through the water*

Right   *A "bayou" or backwater. The mosses and lichens hanging from the trees are produced by the hot, wet climate*

9872

Greek-style houses in which they used to live. In contrast to these beautiful homes, we also see the hovels in which the Negro slaves were kept. There is still a great deal of poverty in the southern states. This is not just found in the Negro population; there are some very poor whites as well. If we take a tour of Natchez we will see both extremes of wealth and poverty.

The Negroes have had a very hard struggle to gain their freedom in the South. When they were slaves life was hard although most were well treated by their masters. When the South lost the Civil War in the 1860s, the Negroes were freed. This sounds good, but there were drawbacks. They had no education, no money of their own and had never had to fend for themselves. They were given land to farm, but with no money how could they do well? The result was that many of them were exploited by the whites. Most of these whites came from the north – the very people who had fought for the freedom of the slaves.

On our way from Natchez to Baton Rouge we

Above *Baton Rouge and the Mississippi*

pass one of the most interesting features of man's interference with the river. Just below the border between Mississippi state and Louisiana, Old River joins the Mississippi. Some years ago the Mississippi tried to change its course, taking a shorter route to the sea by way of the River Atchafalaya. Apart from the damage that this would have caused to all the land and towns along the Atchafalaya, it would have meant disaster for Baton Rouge and New Orleans. They would be left without a river, without the artery for their business, and so without income.

On a map it looks as if the water in Old River is flowing into the Mississippi, but the opposite is the case. The Mississippi flows into Old River, or at least part of it does. This "part" has been getting larger every year. Engineers knew that it could not be allowed to become too large a part of the Mississippi or it would be impossible to do anything to stop it.

In the early 1950s it was clear that danger was close. What should they do? They decided to build sluice gates across Old River. These can be opened in times of high water and closed during normal flow to make sure the Mississippi stays on course. There is a large lock to enable boats to take the shorter route to the Gulf of Mexico, but the Mississippi itself must go the long way round.

Baton Rouge is today one of the greatest oil towns in the world. Along the river bank we see hundreds of oil tanks beside which ships and barges line up to empty or fill their holds. Pipelines carry petroleum products to the interior of the United States from the refineries.

The Mississippi is essential to the oil industry. It takes about 7,300 litres (1,600 gallons) of water to refine one barrel of crude oil. The river provides enough water to refine 340,000 barrels a day.

On the way to New Orleans we pass Bonnet Carré, another floodway used to take water from the Mississippi in times of flood. Because of the many channels in the delta, the main river gets smaller as it nears the end of its journey, helped by the engineers' methods of flood control.

Below *A barge carrying oil pipes being pushed along the river near New Orleans*

New Orleans and the Delta

At last we have reached the famous city of New Orleans. It is a charming city, with narrow streets, quaint houses with iron-trellised balconies, cafés and old shops. All these are in the old part of the city, the French Quarter, or Vieux Carré. This is the city where jazz was born. Famous musicians such as Louis Armstrong rose to fame here. Today the city is still full of music which can be heard drifting out of bars and cafés.

Here it was that Abraham Lincoln, who later became president of the United States, first saw slaves sold. The sight shocked and distressed him enormously and continued to distress him long afterwards. It was Lincoln who, as president, gave the slaves their freedom at last.

The New Orleans Mardi Gras ("fat Tuesday") is one of the most famous celebrations in America. This takes place just before Lent, starts

Left *Bourbon Street, New Orleans. The buildings with their balconies are typical of the old French part of the city*

LOUISIANA   MISSISSIPPI

Baton Rouge

New Orleans

LOUISIANA   MISSISSIPPI

DELTA

Delta National Wildlife Refuge

GULF OF   MEXICO

around Christmas with a series of private parties and then bursts into the streets with parades, dancing and masquerade balls. People from all over the world visit New Orleans for Mardi Gras; to get hotel rooms they have to book months in advance.

The motto of New Orleans is "Under my wings everything prospers" and this seems to be true. But would it be so if it were not for the presence of the mighty Mississippi? I think not.

New Orleans is the third largest port in the United States. Without the trade and industry brought by the Mississippi, the city would not survive.

We leave our barge at New Orleans, but have not yet reached the mouth of the river. We are now in the delta area and can explore the network of waterways and swamps which spread out like a spider's web. To do this we shall take a small boat.

The skyline of New Orleans, the third largest port of the United States

56

Above *A coypu – a large rodent that can become a pest when it destroys undergrowth*

The waters are often shallow here and full of weed, tree-stumps and other hidden dangers. A boat with a propeller would not get far. So, the method of travel they use here is a boat with a strange-looking machine mounted on the back. This machine is a huge, fan-like structure encased in wire netting. This pushes the boat forward by sucking air through the fan. It is rather noisy, but we shall be able to go into small creeks and up backwaters which we could not otherwise reach, even using oars.

In days gone by, this area was used as a hiding place. Buccaneers, pirates and murderers once hid here with their treasures. Many of these rascals came from the Caribbean. The delta provided an excellent place for their contacts with traders in the United States. It is easy to see how they could have hidden themselves safely here.

Except at the beginning of our journey, we have not so far seen a great variety of wildlife. Now things are different. In prehistoric times mastodons, elephants and other large animals lived in the delta. Although they are no longer here, of course, there are others whose size will amaze us – frogs as big as footballs, fish called sturgeon nearly 3 m (10 ft) long. There are eels that migrate to the Sargasso Sea in the Atlantic. They lay their eggs there and then die, leaving their hatched young to return to the Mississippi delta.

Many other kinds of fish living here, including a special dogfish, are found only in this area. Alligators are fairly common, so we shall not be going for a swim without keeping careful watch! The coypu, mink, raccoon, river otter, bobcat and white-tail deer all live here. But the wildlife we will notice most are the birds. This whole area plays a key role in the life cycle of American birds. Over 300 species, from eagles and egrets to tiny humming birds, use the delta at some time during the year. In winter, millions of mallard, wood duck and other birds use these waters

Below *Coming in to land – an egret alights in the treetops*

59

Below *The water hyacinth, which spread so fast that it once threatened the fish life of the delta region*

producer in the United States.

There is one plant growing here which is nothing but a nuisance. This is the water hyacinth. It was first planted in 1884 as a present to the United States from Brazil. The people who planted it did not realize what they were doing. The water hyacinth grew at an amazing rate. As the years went by, the flowers covered the water, forming an immense swampy area. The fish found it very hard to survive and the waters became impossible to sail through. As fast as the engineers removed the weed it grew again, even more strongly. Its control now costs the United States about 70 million dollars a year.

The Mississippi meets the sea 160 km (100 miles) from New Orleans. It has had a long journey, sometimes exciting, sometimes dangerous, sometimes mysterious and always interesting. Its great power has been quashed by the engineers; part of its mystery has been removed. It is no longer allowed to rampage unchecked through the countryside.

We have seen what can happen when Man takes on Nature to ensure his own survival; we have also seen what can happen if Nature gets the upper hand. If all the sums have been done correctly, if Nature continues to behave as it has in the past, if . . .

No-one can be sure the Mississippi will not flood again; we can only be sure that as long as rain continues to fall, water will flow to the sea. The Mississippi will always be here – or there – or there!

on their way south to warmer climates. And, of course, where you find wild duck you find sportsmen trying to shoot them. People from all over the state come here in winter for the hunt.

The Mississippi pours thousands of tonnes of silt into the sea every year. Each year the delta grows a further 100 m (110 yds) out into the sea. The silty water is full of things which fish like to eat. This has made the great salt marshes of Louisiana's coast the most important seafood

Above *A reminder of the strength of the mighty Mississippi, here seen flooding in Louisiana. Over the years* 61
engineers have learned to control its waters, but it is still a forceful power of Nature

Glossary

Artery A vitally important supply route (like the arteries which carry blood through our bodies).
Barge Flat-bottomed boat for carrying cargo.
Barrow Grave-mound containing bodies covered with earth.
Basin Area of country drained by a river and its tributaries.
Cotton baron A man made rich by growing and selling cotton.
Creek Short arm or inlet of a river.
Dam Man-made barrier across a river, large enough to form a lake behind it.
Delta Triangular-shaped land at the mouth of a river.
Dredging Clearing mud from the bottom of a river.
Dyke A ditch: a long embankment or earth-bank.
Fathom A measure of 1.8 m (6 ft), used for measuring depth of water.
Floodway A passage for taking flood water.
Geology Study of the make-up of the earth's crust.
Great Lakes Lakes Superior, Michigan, Huron, Erie and Ontario in North America.
Hydro-electric power Electricity produced using the power of water.
Levee A bank built up at the river's edge to prevent flooding.

Lock Walled-in section of a canal where water levels can be changed for raising and lowering boats.
Logging Industry of cutting down trees for timber.
Malaria A disease causing fever which is carried by the malarial mosquito.
Plantation Area planted with crops, trees etc.
Reef A ridge of rock, shingle or sand just above or below the surface of water.
Refinery Place where raw materials are purified.
River pilot Person who guides boats up and down dangerous parts of a river.
Silt Fine fragments of soil and rock carried down in river water.
Slavery Use of people for work without payment.
Sluice gate Gate across a river or canal to control its flow.
Snag boat A boat used on the Mississippi for removing objects in the river which might be a danger to river traffic.
Sounding Measuring the depth of water.
Swamp Wet, spongy ground.
Tributary River or stream that runs into another, often larger, one.
TVA Tennessee Valley River Authority.
Wagon train Group of horse-drawn covered wagons.

Further Reading

Finley, D. *The Mississippi* (Macdonald Educational, 1975)

Grove, Noel "Mark Twain, Mirror of America" in *National Geographic* volume 148, no. 3, (1975) pages 300–339

Knauth, Percy *The American North Woods* (Time Life Books, 1975)

Lauber, Patricia *The Mississippi, Giant at Work* (Garrard, 1961)

Miller, A. (ed.) *The Mississippi – The Life and Legends of America's Greatest River* (Orbis, 1975)

Twain, Mark *Life on the Mississippi* (first published 1883)

Twain, Mark *Adventures of Huckleberry Finn* (Puffin Books, Penguin, 1970)

Twain, Mark *Adventures of Tom Sawyer* (Puffin Books, Penguin, 1970)

ACKNOWLEDGEMENTS

American History Picture Library, *frontispiece*, 12, 26, 37, 46, 61; Keith Anderson, 35, 54; Ardea London, 16 *right* (Tom Willock), 19 (J. Swedborg), 44 (Elizabeth S. Burgess), 58 (I. and L. Beames), 59 (J. Swedborg), 60 (Kenneth W. Fink); Barnaby's Picture Library, 28, 36, 43; Camera Press, 18, 51; Bruce Coleman, 45 (George Laycock); Robert Harding, 23; Eric Hosking, 48; NASA, 9; Picturepoint, 31, 42, 50; Popperfoto, 49, 52, 53, 57; Spectrum, 40–1, 56; US Army Corps of Engineers, 8, 14, 20, 22, 24, 27; Western Americana Picture Library, 11, 13, 16 *left*, 17, 29, 30, 32, 34, 38. Artwork by Alan Gunston, Michael Paysden and Celia Ware.

Facts and Figures

Size of Mississippi basin: 3,211,000 sq km (1,244,000 sq miles).

Length: 3,800 km (2,375 miles).

Length of the Mississippi/Missouri: 6,400 km (4,000 miles).

Average rate of flow: 18,802 cu m (664,000 cu ft) per second. Rate of flow at times of high water can be twice this figure.

Silt deposits: The Mississippi deposits 359 million cu m (12,700 million cu ft) of silt each year, of which 14 million cu m (500 million cu ft) forms the delta on the Gulf of Mexico. Each year the land in the Gulf extends a further 100 m (110 yd) into the sea.

Trade: Total annual weight of goods carried on the Mississippi and its tributaries is 203 million tonnes (200 million tons). This figure is increasing as industry increases.

Rate of fall: The Mississippi only falls 450 m (1,475 ft) from source to mouth. From St. Louis to the delta it falls only 82 m (270 ft).

Floods: Very bad floods occurred in 1882, 1884, 1890, 1891, 1897, 1898, 1903, 1912, 1913, 1916 and 1927.

Ports: The main ports of the Mississippi are New Orleans, Baton Rouge and Memphis.

Index

Appalachian Mountains 10, 36
Arkansas 12, 47
Arkansas River 47
Atchafalaya River 52

Baton Rouge 51, 52, 53
Bonnet Carré 53

Cairo 33, 35
California 30
Cavalier, Robert 12
Clark, William 29

Delta (town of) 48
disease 11, 30, 36

Effigy Mounds 26

farming 18, 21, 27, 28, 36, 39, 40
Fontana Dam 36
fur trappers 16, 26, 29

Grafton 28
Great Lakes 10, 28
Gulf of Mexico 9, 10, 53

Hannibal 26

Ice Age 10
Illinois 21, 35
Illinois River 28
Iowa 25

Jolliet, Louis 11

Kansas City 29
Knoxville 36

La Crosse 25
Lake Bemidji 18
Lake Itasca 10, 15, 18
Le Moyne, Jean Baptiste 12
Lewis, Merriweather 29
Lincoln, Abraham 55
Logging 18
Louis XV 12
Louisiana 12, 52, 60
Louisiana Purchase 12, 29

McGregor 26
Marquette, Jacques 11
Memphis 40, 47
Minneapolis 18, 21, 22
Minnesota 10, 16, 21, 25
Minnesota River 25
Mississippi 47, 52
Mississippi River
    barges 12, 22, 25, 27, 33
    basin 10
    buried cities 40
    canals 12, 18
    course changes 35, 40, 48, 52
    dams 12, 22, 36, 48
    delta 53, 56, 58, 59
    explorers 10, 11, 12, 15, 29
    flood control 12, 28, 36, 48, 52, 53
    floods 9, 12, 40
    industry of 12, 43, 52, 53, 56
    length 9, 10
    levees 39, 44, 48
    mouth 56, 60
    other names 9, 11
    silt 10, 28, 44, 60
    source 10, 15
    transport 12, 33, 36, 43, 44
    tributaries 9, 25, 28, 35, 36, 47
    use as boundary 25, 35
    width 9, 18, 33, 43, 44
Missouri 35
Missouri River 10, 28, 30

Missouri River Authority 28

Napoleon Bonaparte 12
Natchez 48
New Madrid 40
New Orleans 12, 43, 52, 55

Ohio River 35, 36
Old River 52
Oregon 30

Pennsylvania 36
Prairie du Chien 26
President Jefferson 29

Quebec 11, 12

Red Indians 9, 15, 18, 26, 30
Rocky Mountains 10, 28, 30

St. Anthony's Falls 18
St. Croix River 25
St. Louis 22, 29, 30
St. Paul 21
Schoolcraft, Henry Rowe 15
Settlers 21, 29, 30
Slaves 9, 35, 39, 40, 48, 55
de Soto, Hernando 10, 11
Steamboats 33, 47
Sultana 47

Tennessee 47
Tennessee River 36
Tennessee Valley River Authority 36
Twain, Mark 26

Vicksburg 48

Wildlife 16, 25, 59
Wisconsin 25
Wisconsin River 12

The Mississippi